Terrorism

DEBATING
THE ISSUES

Terrorism

JON
STERNGASS

mc Marshall Cavendish
Benchmark
New York

Published by Marshall Cavendish Benchmark
An imprint of Marshall Cavendish Corporation

4913 7275 3/12

Other Marshall Cavendish Offices:
Marshall Cavendish International (Asia) Private Limited, 1 New Industrial Road, Singapore 536196 •
Marshall Cavendish International (Thailand) Co Ltd. 253 Asoke, 12th Flr, Sukhumvit 21 Road, Klongtoey
Nua, Wattana, Bangkok 10110, Thailand • Marshall Cavendish (Malaysia) Sdn Bhd, Times Subang,
Lot 46, Subang Hi-Tech Industrial Park, Batu Tiga, 40000 Shah Alam, Selangor Darul Ehsan, Malaysia

Marshall Cavendish is a trademark of Times Publishing Limited

All websites were available and accurate when this book was sent to press.

Library of Congress Cataloging-in-Publication Data

Sterngass, Jon.
   Terrorism / Jon Sterngass.
       p. cm. — (Debating the issues)
   Includes bibliographical references and index.
   ISBN 978-0-7614-4977-5 (print)—ISBN 978-1-60870-667-9 (ebook)
   1. Terrorism—Juvenile literature. I. Title. II. Series.

   HV6431.S743 2012
   363.325—dc22

   2010039512

Editor: Peter Mavrikis
Publisher: Michelle Bisson
Art Director: Anahid Hamparian
Series design by Sonia Chaghatzbanian

Photo research by Alison Morretta

The photographs in this book are used by permission and through the courtesy of:
Front cover: Greg Martin/Superstock.
Alamy: Blue Shadows, 1, 2-3, 4-5. **Associated Press:** Associated Press, 10, 16, 34; Yahya Ahmed, 14;
Press Association, 22; Santiago Lyon, 25; Radar Bali, 41; Greg Baker, 44; Handout, 46; Ted S. Warren,
52; Dmitry Lovetsky, 69. *Getty Images:* Jerry Cooke/Sports Illustrated, 6; John Hoagland, 11; Robert
Nickelsberg, 13; Georges DeKeerle, 17; Bob Houlihan/U.S. Navy, 19; Anton Denisov/AFP, 26; Alexander
Joe/AFP, 28; Japanese Defense Agency, 31; Bob Daemmrich/AFP, 32; Alexandre-Francois Caminade,
38; Erik S. Lesser, 48; Joshua Roberts/AFP, 50; Mario Tama, 55; AFP, 59; Reza, 65; Seyllou/AFP, 72.
Superstock: Age Fotostock, 56; Visions of America, 62.
Back cover: Science Faction/Superstock.

Printed in Malaysia (T)
135642

Table of Contents

Chapter 1

On September 5, 1972, the Munich Summer Olympic Games were already into their second week. The host nation, West Germany, had gone out of its way to encourage an open and friendly atmosphere in the Olympic Village. The German hosts did not want to revive memories of the Nazi past and World War II.

On that morning, a group of armed Palestinians, taking advantage of the relaxed security in the Olympic Village, climbed a fence and gained access to the Israeli athletes' dormitory. They killed two Israelis immediately and took nine **hostages**. In exchange for the hostages' lives, the attackers demanded the release of 234 Palestinian prisoners jailed in Israel; they also demanded to be flown to Egypt. In response, German security forces set up an **ambush** at the airport. The Germans had no training in dealing with a hostage situation, however, and the rescue attempt failed. As the world watched the events on television, sharpshooters succeeded in killing five of the kidnappers but all nine athletes were also killed in the gun battle.

The Germans captured three of the Palestinian hostage takers but released them in a deal following the Palestinian hijacking of a German airplane later in the year. The Palestinians received a hero's welcome

Flags fly at half mast at the Munich Olympics in 1972 in memory of the Israeli athletes killed by Palestinians.

in Libya. Israel responded to the killings in Munich with a series of air strikes and assassinations that targeted anyone involved in planning the kidnapping. The Israeli revenge missions continued for more than twenty years.

The bloody events at the 1972 Munich Olympics ushered in an age of terrorism that continues to this day. From that time on, it became impossible to ignore an increase in the number of attacks, **hijackings**, and suicide bombings. Since then, terrorists have planted bombs on busy streets and in shopping areas. They have blown up planes, trains, and ferries. They have taken people hostage in schools and theaters.

Terrorists have been known to use spectacular tactics to bring international attention to their cause. Such tactics are not always successful, but the Munich incident did benefit the Palestinians. Before 1972, almost no one knew anything about the Palestinians. After the Munich Olympics, hundreds of millions of people knew something of their struggle for independence. A Palestinian representative at the United Nations said, "The first several hijackings accomplished more for the [Palestinian] cause than twenty years of pleading at the United Nations."

Modern terrorism is a technique used by people of different nationalities and religions. Terrorist **tactics** appear all over the world and are used by people to achieve many different goals. The U.S. National Counterterrorism Center estimates that there were 14,506 terrorist attacks in 2007 and 11,770 terrorist attacks in 2008. Worldwide, more than 15,000 people died because of terrorism in 2008 (19 American citizens) and more than 20,000 in 2007 (33 American citizens).

Difficulty in Defining Terrorism

There is no accepted definition of the word *terrorism*. One study came up with 109 separate definitions of terrorism, offered by governments and scholars. Many of the definitions differed a great deal from one another.

Calling someone a terrorist is a political form of name-calling. It is common to label any particularly violent act as "terrorism." Whether a person is called an underground soldier or a terrorist often depends on the point of view of the person assigning the label. Menachem Begin (Prime Minister of Israel, 1977-1983), Nelson Mandela (President of South Africa, 1994-1999), and Yasser Arafat (President of the Palestinian National Authority, 1996-2004) were at one time labeled terrorists—yet all won Nobel Peace Prizes later in their lives. Leaders once dubbed terrorists, such as Jomo Kenyatta (President of Kenya) and Gerry Adams (President of Sinn Féin, a political party in Northern Ireland), became national and internationally accepted figures.

In fact, both the British Broadcasting Company (BBC) and Al Jazeera, the Arabic television news network, avoid the use of the words *terrorism* or *terrorist*. An editor of the BBC explained, "It is the style of the BBC World Service to call no one a terrorist aware as we are that one man's terrorist is another one's freedom fighter." Instead of *terrorism* and *terrorists*, newsreaders refer to *attacks, bombings, fighters, militants,* and *insurgents*.

When people agree with the goals of the killers, they tend to be more tolerant of the death of **civilians**. In the United States, one study showed that an act of political violence was far more likely to be labeled

Yassir Arafat (1929-2004): Palestinian leader, accused terrorist, Nobel Peace Prize winner.

"terrorism" if an American citizen was a victim. Most of the world considers the Irish Republican Army to be terrorists, but to some residents of Northern Ireland, they are heroes because they fight British **oppression**. The U.S. government labels Hamas a terrorist organization yet many Palestinians view it is a legitimate political party and resistance movement to occupation. At the same time, the United States has supported, financed, and trained groups that are widely viewed by other countries as terrorist, such as the contras in Nicaragua, the mujahideen in Afghanistan, UNITA in Angola, and Samuel K. Doe in Liberia.

Nor has the United Nations (UN) been able to define the problem. More than ten major multinational agreements detail a country's responsibilities to fight terrorism. However, UN members have never agreed on a definition of terrorism, and disputes commonly arise as to who are the victims and who are the **aggressors**.

Nicaraguan "contras" in 1983. The United States called them freedom fighters, though many others viewed them as terrorists who intentionally killed civilians.

Defining Terrorism

There are several possible component parts of a definition of terrorism. Most definitions have three or four common elements: (1) the use of violence; (2) the existence of political objectives; (3) the intention of causing fear in a target population; and (4) the willingness to attack civilians, or **noncombatants**.

Terrorists use violence or the threat of violence, but the tactic is not just about death and destruction. The word itself comes from the Latin word *terrere*, which means "to frighten." Terrorist tactics aim to create fear and suspicion, undermine public confidence, and provoke people and governments into doing things that they might otherwise not do. Terrorists use violence to achieve political change. Without some political goal, they would simply be mass murderers.

Labeling an action "terrorism" is essentially a matter of perception. The distinction between a terrorist act and a legitimate act of guerrilla warfare is not always clear. However, acts of terrorism are usually not ends in themselves. It is a matter of complete indifference to the terrorist whether the particular victims of a terrorist action live or die. The more important goal for terrorists is getting their message across to a larger audience.

Many definitions of terrorism emphasize the aspect of its being a deliberate attack on innocent people, civilians, or noncombatants. If this part of the definition is adopted, then targeting soldiers, judges, police, or local collaborators would not count as acts of terrorism because the victims are not "innocent." In the same way, an **assassin** would not truly be a terrorist. Assassins target and murder individuals not randomly but because of who they are. However, because political leaders are considered noncombatants under international law, some definitions of terrorism include the act of political assassination.

State Terrorism

Terrorism is often used by people without a regular army against the power of a major country. However, governments sometimes use terrorist-style tactics against their opponents within a country.

The Muslim mujahideen helped expel Soviet invaders from Afghanistan in the 1980s.
The U.S. called the mujahideen "freedom fighters" when they fought Russians, but
"terrorists" when some of them became the Taliban and fought Americans.

These tactics include killing, torture, and kidnapping followed by "disappearance." Some examples include the use of death squads in Argentina (1976–1983) and El Salvador (1980–1983) and the use of gas against Kurds by the Iraqi government (1988). In the Soviet Union (especially 1930–1951) and Nazi Germany (1933–1945), state terror was a basic part of keeping the people intimidated and the government in power. In those two countries, state terrorism gradually changed into mass murder and genocide, and the result was the deaths of millions of people.

Another form of state terrorism occurs during wartime. For thousands of years, armies have murdered civilians to weaken the morale of their

State terrorism kills far more people than nongovernmental terrorism. A man places flowers on the grave of a victim killed in a 1988 chemical attack by the Iraqi government on it own Kurdish citizens.

enemies and convince them to surrender. Strategic bombing in World War II was based on the idea of terrorizing civilian populations with massive air attacks to compel their governments to surrender. In the most extreme case, in 1945, the United States chose Hiroshima and Nagasaki as the targets of atomic bombs specifically because the two cities had no military significance. More than 200,000 people were killed. It was hardly different from sending American soldiers door-to-door, with orders to randomly shoot everyone. On the other hand, some argued that atomic weapons were in essence just a refinement of **conventional war**.

A third form of state terrorism occurs when a government uses violence against noncombatants as a tactic of foreign policy. For example, in 1987, North Korean agents blew up Korean Air Flight 858; all 115 people on the plane were killed. The North Korean government had wanted to disrupt upcoming elections in South Korea and frighten sports teams from attending the Seoul Summer Olympics. In another case the same year, 1988, Libyan agents killed 270 people when they blew up Pan Am Flight 103 over Lockerbie, Scotland. Fifteen years later, Libya formally admitted responsibility and offered $2.7 billion compensation to victims' families.

History of Terrorism

Terrorism is a very old tactic. The massacre of the inhabitants

> # DID YOU KNOW?
> The U.S. Department of State annually puts out a list of what it considers terrorist nations. As of 2011, the four countries on the list were Cuba, Sudan, Iran, and Syria. Libya was removed from the list in 2006 and North Korea in 2008. However, this list has often been criticized as being driven more by American foreign and domestic policy than actual evaluation of support for terrorism.

It can still be terrorism even at 22,000 feet (6,700 m). Two German bombers target British cities in an attempt to destroy civilian morale in 1940 in World War II.

Officials inspect the wreckage of Flight 103, which exploded over Lockerbie, Scotland, in 1988, killing 270 people. In 2003, Libya formally admitted responsibility for the bombing and offered $2.7 billion to the victims' families.

of a captured city used to be a common feature of warfare. A general could make conquests easier by proclaiming that cities that refused to yield immediately would be razed and their inhabitants killed.

Organized assassination also has a long history. In first-century Judea, Jewish Zealots used assassination as a strategy to fight Roman occupation. In the eleventh century, a Shiite sect attacked Christian officials and Sunni opponents. This group was known as the Nizari or Ismaili but is commonly called the Assassins.

Until the 1800s, however, state terrorism was the most common form of terrorism. The model for a government turning on its own citizens was associated with the Reign of Terror during the French Revolution (1793–1794), a period of mass executions of political suspects. This association changed during the nineteenth century when nongovernmental groups such as **anarchists** and **nationalists** began to preach "propaganda of the deed." They realized that acts of violence helped groups gain publicity. However, the targets of these attacks were usually political opponents and not civilians.

After World War II (1939–1945), the use of terrorist tactics spread to many nongovernmental organizations. Some were fighting for independence against colonial overlords; others wanted to separate from an already existing independent nation. In the 1960s and 1970s, radical **Marxist** groups in Europe adopted violence as a way to fight the power of capitalist governments.

After the Munich Olympics, the range of groups and national states using terrorist tactics became so wide that it is impossible to generalize. The most popular recent use of terrorist tactics is by fundamentalist religious groups, especially by radical Muslims who oppose the political and cultural influence of non-Muslims and the Western world. Members of Al Qaeda, a group of this type, are widely believed to be responsible for the hijacking of four commercial passenger airliners and using them to destroy the World Trade Center in New York City and other targets in September 2001. Almost 3,000 people died in the attack, by far the bloodiest nongovernmental terrorist action in history.

The American military headquarters known as the Pentagon was a target in Al Qaeda's attack on the United States in 2001. This 200-foot (60 m) gash resulted when a hijacked commercial airliner crashed into the Washington, D.C., building.

WHAT DO YOU THINK?

Can you write your own definition of *terrorism* in two sentences or less?

In 1983, suicide bombers blew up truck bombs in buildings housing the United States and French military forces in Lebanon. This attack was carried out by people who thought the U.S. military presence in Lebanon was an invasive influence in their civil war. Almost 250 soldiers died, including 220 U.S. Marines.

GUILT AND INNOCENCE

The costs of terrorist tactics are truly heartbreaking. Television viewers have seen the mangled corpses, the twisted and charred pieces of metal, and the blood scattered over the sites. Relatives scream hysterically and search desperately among the rubble for loved ones. Children are left without parents and parents without children. Hospitals are flooded with injured bodies. People die because they were in the wrong place at the wrong time, because they happened to take the wrong airplane or ferry, attend the wrong school or theater, or dine at the wrong pizza parlor. Outrage and horror are natural reactions to random violence against innocent men, women, and children.

However, the people who commit these acts see them differently. Since the United States is a democracy, Osama bin Laden, the head of Al Qaeda, argued that American citizens could be held collectively responsible for the actions of their government. Bin Laden said, "By electing these leaders, the American people have given their consent to the incarceration of the Palestinian people, the demolition of Palestinian homes. . . . The American people have the ability and choice to refuse the policies of their Government, yet time and again, polls show the American people support the policies of the elected Government. . . . This is why the American people are not innocent."

Another Al Qaeda member responsible for attacks in London in 2005 said, "Your democratically elected governments continuously perpetrate atrocities against my people. . . . And your support of them makes you directly responsible. . . . [O]ur words have no impact upon you therefore I'm going to talk to you in a language that you understand. Our words are dead until we give them life with our blood."

People who use terrorist tactics usually ignore the law. They believe that governments created legal rules to make it impossible for small nongovernmental organizations to defeat large forces. One member of the Shining Path movement in Peru said, "Violence is the only way. Innocent people always die, it's inevitable."

Do you consider this an act of terrorism according to your definition? Why or why not? Do you think sleeping or off-duty military personnel are noncombatants? What other information would you like to have?

People who use terrorist tactics insist, "You cannot make an omelet without breaking eggs." What do you think this expression means? Do you think it is a good argument for the use of terrorist tactics? Why or why not?

Osama bin Laden is despised as a crazed terrorist in the United States but he is revered by many as a hero in the Islamic world. Is he a terrorist? Why or why not?

Chapter 2

Nongovernmental terrorism usually involves a small group of people who wage war on a larger group, such as a government. Terrorist groups want their attacks to be surprises, so they make plans in secret. They rarely have access to military weapons or artillery, so they often use homemade bombs and car bombs and other such unsophisticated devices. They also use grenades, handguns, and assault rifles. Because most terrorist groups do not have a territorial base, they usually try to blend in with civilian populations and do not wear uniforms.

Few groups label themselves "terrorist." Group members are aware of the negative image of the term. An exception is the man who assembled the bomb in the first attack on the World Trade Center (1993); he stated, "Yes, I am a terrorist, and proud of it as long as it is against the U.S. government."

More common is the response of an Irish Republican Army member after being convicted of several attempted murders and kidnapping. "'Terrorist' is a dirty word," he said, "and I certainly don't . . . nor have I ever considered myself to be one . . . I remain an activist to this day."

In 1998, a splinter group of the IRA organized a car bomb attack in Omagh. Twenty-nine people died and about 220 were injured in Northern Ireland's worst single incident of violence.

The groups listed below are all widely considered terrorist organizations. They all have used violence and targeted civilians for political gain. They have killed hundreds and sometimes thousands of noncombatants. However, few of these groups consider themselves to be lawless terrorists. They insist their violence is morally justified and a legitimate response to oppression and terror by the state.

Terrorism and Independence

Some groups want to capture or control land on behalf of a people, culture, or religion. These groups sometimes choose to use terrorist tactics as a strategic method to accomplish their goals. Examples of this link between terrorism and some independence movements are:

Kurdistan Workers Party in the Middle East (PKK)

Euskadi Ta Askatasuna (ETA) in Spain

Chechen separatists in Russia

Irish Republican Army (IRA) in Northern Ireland

Tamil Tigers (LTTE) in Sri Lanka

PKK

The Kurdish people, numbering more than 20 million, are the largest ethnic group without a nation. The PKK desires to create an independent Kurdish state comprising areas of Turkey, Iraq, Syria, and Iran where the Kurdish population is the majority. The PKK suicide bombers have struck government buildings and tourist sites, and the group has assassinated targeted government officials.

ETA

The ETA is fighting for the independence of Spain's northern Basque region. It began in 1959 as a Basque group encouraging traditional cultural ways but evolved into a paramilitary group supporting the use of violence. Since 1968, the ETA has killed more than 800 people and been involved in dozens of kidnappings.

CHECHEN SEPARATISTS

The Chechens are a Muslim ethnic **minority** who live in Russia's Caucasus region. Since 1990, Chechen separatists have fought for the region's independence and

A banner supporting the outlawed Basque separatist group ETA is proudly raised in Spain in 1996. Since 1968, the ETA has killed more than 800 people and been involved in dozens of kidnappings.

been involved in numerous attacks on civilians. In 1999, Chechen bombings of a shopping arcade and apartment building in Moscow killed 64 people. In 2002, Chechen fighters seized a theater in Moscow where about 700 people were attending a performance; more than 120 people died in a rescue attempt.

IRA

In Northern Ireland, the Irish Republican Army (IRA) has fought for the area's independence from Great Britain since 1916. Between 1969 and 1999—a period of conflict called The Troubles—more than 3,000 people died in fighting between Catholics and Protestants. In this period, the IRA was responsible for more than 1,700 deaths, including British police, soldiers, and civilians. The Belfast Agreement of 1998 appeared to end most of the violence. However, a splinter group of the IRA rejected the Belfast Agreement and organized a car bomb attack

In 2002, Chechen separatists attacked a theater in Moscow. A controversial rescue attempt resulted in many deaths but rescued more than 700 hostages. (See Case Study #2 on page 67 for more on this incident.)

in Omagh in 1998. Twenty-nine people died, and about 220 were injured in Northern Ireland's worst single terrorist atrocity.

LTTE

About 13 percent of Sri Lanka's 21 million people are Tamils. The Tamil people are an Indian ethnic group that is primarily Hindu. In Sri Lanka, the vast majority of the population is Sinhalese and Buddhist. The goal of the Tamil Tigers (LTTE), an organization founded in 1976, was to create an independent Tamil state in northeastern Sri Lanka. The resulting civil war lasted more than thirty years and cost almost 100,000 lives. The Tamil Tigers were one of the first groups to use suicide bombing. The LTTE was defeated in 2009; the future of the movement remained uncertain in late 2011.

Terrorism for Political Reasons

Some groups do not want to separate. They use terrorist tactics to replace what they see as a corrupt and useless form of government with another model or ideal. Some groups that fit this model include:

Shining Path in Peru
Armed Islamic Group (GIA) in Algeria
Al Qaeda

THE SHINING PATH

The Shining Path (*Sendero Luminoso*) movement in Peru, founded in the late 1960s, attempted to overthrow the corrupt capitalist government

In 1998, the U.S. embassies in Kenya and Tanzania were attacked by Al Qaeda suicide bombers. More than 300 people were killed and 4,000 wounded. Here, U.S. Secretary of State Madeleine Albright looks at the damage in Tanzania.

of Peru. Between 1980 and 1992, the Shining Path carried out regular violent operations that killed more than 11,000 civilians. One member of the movement said, "Our task is to kill all those who stand in the way of the Shining Path's war." As many as 70,000 people died overall in fighting between the Peruvian government and the Shining Path. The movement declined after its leader, Abimael Guzmán, was captured and imprisoned in 1992.

GIA

The Armed Islamic Group (GIA) is a Muslim organization that wants to overthrow the Algerian government and replace it with an Islamic state. In the 1990s, the GIA conducted a campaign of brutal civilian massacres. In 1997–1998, GIA attacks on Algerian villages, especially Sidi Moussa, Hais Rais, Ben Talha, and Ami Moussa, killed thousands. The GIA's policy of killing civilians was controversial, and the organization has virtually ceased to exist since 2001.

AL QAEDA

Al Qaeda is an international organization that up until May 2011 was led by Osama bin Laden. He established the group in 1988 with Muslims who fought in Afghanistan against the invasion by the Soviet Union. Al Qaeda wants to unite Muslims to overthrow governments that are not Islamic, especially in Asia and the Middle East, and to expel non-Muslims from these countries. Al Qaeda's ultimate goal is to establish Islamic rule—a so-called Islamic caliphate—from Spain to Indonesia.

Al Qaeda believes that the United States has insulted Islam by (1) establishing military bases in the holy land of Saudi Arabia; (2) trying to manipulate Muslim nations in order to get Middle Eastern oil; and (3) continuing to support Israel. The members of Al Qaeda believe these actions constitute a declaration of war against God and therefore justify a holy war against the United States.

Al Qaeda is responsible for numerous violent actions against civilians. The most infamous is the September 11, 2001, attacks by four hijacked American passenger planes. Two of the planes smashed into the twin towers of the World Trade Center, in New York City, a third crashed into the Pentagon, outside Washington, D.C., and a fourth crashed in Pennsylvania. Almost 3,000 people were killed and 9,000 wounded, by far the most casualties of any single terrorist incident.

Al Qaeda is also linked with other incidents:

- The 1998 bombings of the U.S. embassies in Nairobi, Kenya, and Dar es Salaam, Tanzania; 303 killed, 4,000 injured.
- The 2002 suicide bombing of a synagogue in Tunisia; 21 killed, 32 injured.
- The 2004 bomb attacks on Madrid commuter trains; 191 killed and more than 1,800 injured.
- The 2005 bombings of the London public transportation system; 56 killed, more than 700 injured.

In addition, Al Qaeda is suspected of having carried out or having directed sympathetic groups to carry out the following attacks:

- The 1993 World Trade Center bombing in New York City; 6 killed, more than 1,000 injured.
- The 2002 nightclub bombing in Bali, Indonesia; 202 killed, 350 injured.
- The 2004 Philippine ferry bombing near Manila, 116 killed.

As American as Apple Pie

At about 9 a.m. on April 19, 1995, a homemade car bomb exploded outside the Alfred P. Murrah Federal Building in Oklahoma City, Oklahoma. The powerful blast collapsed the walls and floors of the building,

WEAPONS OF MASS DESTRUCTION AND TERRORISM

The term *weapons of mass destruction* refers to chemical, biological, or nuclear weapons. A simple fertilizer bomb can cause enormous casualties, as in the bombing of the Alfred P. Murrah Federal Building in Oklahoma City in 1995. If terrorists were to use weapons of mass destruction, the cost in civilian casualties would be impossible to calculate beforehand.

The most notable attack with chemical weapons took place in Tokyo in 1995. Twelve people died and 5,500 were injured when several packages left in moving subway cars began to spurt a powerful **nerve gas**. Aum Shinrikyo, a religious cult that believed that the end of the world was coming soon, organized the attack, possibly as a way of bringing down the Japanese government and hastening the apocalypse.

When asked if terrorist groups might use weapons of mass destruction (WMDs) against civilian targets, a former U.S. Secretary of Defense said, "It isn't a question of 'if,' but 'when.'" After Al Qaeda's attacks on September 11, 2001,

Japanese workers clear the remains of Sarin nerve gas off a Tokyo subway platform after the 1995 gas attack by a Japanese cult. Twelve people were killed and more than 5,000 injured.

the allegation that Iraq had WMDs was used by President George W. Bush to justify the invasion of that country in 2003. It is now beyond dispute that Iraq did not possess any WMDs or have meaningful ties to Al Qaeda.

However, in an interview in 1999, Osama bin Laden (1957-2011) did say that acquiring chemical and nuclear weapons "for the defense of Muslims is a religious duty. If I have indeed acquired these weapons, then I thank God for enabling me to do so. . . . It would be a sin for Muslims not to try to possess the weapons." It is not clear whether bin Laden was using psychological warfare or actually had these weapons or intended to try to get them.

Timothy McVeigh, an American militia movement supporter, was executed for his involvement in the 1995 truck bombing of the Federal Building in Oklahoma City that killed 168 people.

and 168 people died, including 19 small children. Two Americans had blown up the building to avenge what they thought were attacks by the U.S. government against the American people.

Americans sometimes think of terrorists as foreigners. However, American history is filled with terrorist groups. For more than a hundred years, the Ku Klux Klan targeted blacks in the South. They murdered black people and

DID YOU KNOW?

In 1920 in New York City, a bomb planted in an unattended horse-drawn wagon on Wall Street exploded. Thirty-five people were killed and hundreds more injured. The person or persons responsible for the bombing were never identified.

set fire to homes, schools, and businesses owned by blacks.

Modern American hate groups continue to target blacks as well as Jews, Asians, and other immigrants. Many of them despise the American government. They collect guns and urge their members to kill anyone connected with the government. People sympathetic to this movement were responsible for the Oklahoma City bombing.

Antiabortion violence is another form of American terrorism. Radical groups and individuals opposed to the procedure attack people and places that provide abortions. Their violent acts have included bombing abortion clinics and murdering doctors, nurses, and health-care workers at women's clinics. Two examples involved the murder of doctors: Dr. Barnett Slepian was killed in 1998—shot through a window in his house in upstate New York—and Dr. George Tiller was murdered while attending church in Kansas in 2009. One antiabortion extremist said that "executing abortion providers was a moral imperative. . . . Abortion is murder, and murderers deserve to be executed."

WHAT DO YOU THINK?

Why do you think that most groups refuse to identify themselves as "terrorist"?

Why do you think that groups trying to achieve independence often use terrorist tactics?

What are the goals of Al Qaeda? Why does the organization hate the United States?

Chapter 3

After the attacks of September 11, 2001, President George W. Bush said, "We fight against poverty because hope is an answer to terror." Yet the popular stereotype that people who use terrorist tactics are poorer or less educated than the rest of the population is not true. Many studies have shown that there is only a weak link between poverty and membership in a terrorist group.

Many of the groups' leaders are well-off people who intentionally choose a dangerous life of struggle and sacrifice. Abimael Guzmán, the leader of Peru's Shining Path, grew up in a wealthy household and worked as a college professor. Osama bin Laden is extremely affluent from his family's construction business in Saudi Arabia. Velupillai Prabhakaran, the founder of the Tamil Tigers, was a shy, bookish student from a middle-class family. All claimed to be fighting for the rights of the dispossessed, the oppressed, and the underdog.

No common personality profile exists that can distinguish terrorists from other people. The stereotype of terrorists as insane, irrational, or crazed fanatics is also untrue. Most studies have shown no hint of psychological disorder.

Terrorists in a group sacrifice their individual identity to the will

Osama bin Laden (1957-2011) in 1998. The Saudi Arabian is head of Al Qaeda and has been accused of planning numerous terrorist attacks over the last fifteen years.

of the group. They believe that what helps the organization is more important than their own personal happiness. They rarely repent, even when captured. "We are convinced that we will triumph," said one imprisoned member of the Shining Path, "and for that cause we are prepared to give our lives." In many places around the world, young people learn that joining a terrorist group is a normal step that gives life meaning. One member of Hamas explained his membership by saying, "Everyone was joining." The younger people are when they join a terrorist organization, the harder it is to convince them to leave it.

The Role of Religion

The extent of the relationship between religion and the use of terrorist tactics is a matter of controversy. There are those that link deeply felt religious belief to violence against civilians. Others point out that terrorism is usually associated with economic and political grievances. Though they might be expressed through religious speech, they are not religious in nature.

Terrorism occurs in many different cultures, some religious and some not. The Tamil Tigers and Kurdistan Workers Party are not religious, yet they often used suicide bombers. Both organizations found plenty of volunteers without promising them an eternal afterlife. The Provisional Irish Republican Army worked for the Catholic cause in Northern Ireland, but usually expressed its complaints in economic and political terms.

However, extreme religious belief does seem linked to terrorism on some level. Religion provides personal rewards, such as the promise of heaven, to those who fight in conflicts that would otherwise have only social benefits. One female suicide bomber fighting for Chechnya's independence said, "I know what I am doing, paradise has a price, and I hope this will be the price for Paradise."

Christianity's critics accuse it of having a long history of justifying violence, inquisitions, crusades, and attacks on civilian populations. However, in the last forty years, the focus of debate has been on the suggested link between terrorism and Islam. Nevertheless, President George W. Bush said, "These acts of violence against innocents violate the fundamental tenets of the Islamic faith. . . . The face of terror is not the true faith of Islam. That's not what Islam is all about. Islam is peace." Yet others say that modern terrorism is based on or justified by doctrines and beliefs of Islam, such as the high value placed on **martyrdom** and **jihad** (often translated as "holy war").

Terrorist tactics have also caused a sharp debate in the Muslim world. It has been both condemned and supported on religious grounds. Prominent leaders differ sharply in their legal opinions. Some see it as necessary and justified; others see it as murder.

DID YOU KNOW?

Sometimes members of less mainstream religions also use terrorist tactics. In 1985, Sikh extremists blew up Air India Flight 182 in Canadian air space; 329 people were killed. It was the single deadliest terrorist attack involving an aircraft to that date and still represents the largest mass murder in modern Canadian history.

Between 1095 and 1300, Christian soldiers from Europe repeatedly invaded and tried to conquer territory in the Middle East. These religious wars were called the Crusades.

The debate over the place of terrorist tactics in Islam is heated, extremely complex, and far beyond the scope of this book. However, it is worth noting that, historically, both Sunni and Shiite Muslims have forbidden acts of suicide and terrorism.

Random versus Targeted Terrorist Attacks

Sometimes terrorists choose random targets to cause fear and insecurity among people. However, random killing sometimes has a larger purpose. One GIA leader in Algeria proclaimed that "in our war, there is no neutrality. Except for those who are with us, all others are renegades." This was the excuse for attacking thousands of civilians in Algerian villages.

Another purpose of random targeting is to provoke government **counterterrorism** measures; that is, terrorist groups may try to get the government to overreact. For example, in 1985, the Tamil Tigers opened fire on crowds waiting for buses in Anuradhapura, Sri Lanka. This incident, in which 146 people died, was designed to provoke massive retaliation by the Sinhalese majority against the Tamils. The Tigers felt this would ultimately strengthen their position with the Tamil people.

Occasionally, a government's response to a terrorist attack is worse than the attack itself. As a result of the attack, citizens may be subjected to brutality and to the reduction of their civil liberties. This response often convinces local people to support the group fighting against the government. In the 1990s, the president of Peru suspended all constitutional rights in an attempt to defeat the Shining Path. The government used military force that often exceeded the Shining Path in its brutality. This made it much harder for the Peruvian government to defeat the Shining Path.

Some terrorist targets are carefully chosen to support bargaining or to make a political statement. Al Qaeda planned its 2004 attack on the Madrid train station to take place only ten days before national elections in Spain. The bombing was intended to force the Spanish government to withdraw from Iraq or else lead to the defeat of the government in the election.

During the 1990s, the GIA intentionally killed many journalists during Algeria's civil war. GIA leaders said that "those who fight against us by the pen will die by the sword." They considered journalists to be supporters of the government and of a non-Islamic society.

Tourist attractions are also a frequent target of terrorist tactics. In places where tourism is a major source of foreign income, such as Indonesia and Egypt, attacks on tourist sites scare off visitors and weaken the government.

Suicide Bombers

All national states encourage their own people, especially soldiers, to make sacrifices for the general good in times of crisis. Many nations consider people heroes who die to help the country or fellow citizens. The Latin expression *Dulce et decorum est pro patria mori* ("Sweet and fitting it is to die for one's country") has been cited with approval by some Europeans and Americans for centuries.

Suicide bombers are people who willingly sacrifice themselves for a cause. Because suicide bombers do not intend to escape death, they can get close to a crowd and create a great deal of damage. In the last thirty years, many nongovernmental groups have taken up the tactic. As one leader noted, "The person who uses a gun is well trained. The person who explodes a bomb does not need a lot of training—he just needs to have a moment of courage."

Jemaah Islamiyah, a Southeast Asian Islamic organization with links to Al Qaeda, killed 200 and wounded 350 by exploding three bombs outside a nightclub in Bali, Indonesia.

The widespread use of suicide bombers seems to have been revived by Hezbollah in the early 1980s. The Tamil Tigers adopted the tactic in 1987, and then it was taken up by Hamas in Israel, the Kurdistan Workers Party in Turkey, Chechen rebels in Russia, and Al Qaeda throughout the world. Suicide bombing increased in Iraq after the death of Saddam Hussein. Before the U.S. invasion of Iraq in 2003, there had never been a suicide attack in the country's history. Since then, suicide bombers have killed thousands of Iraqis and Americans.

TERRORISM OR RETALIATION?

The targeting of civilians may be retaliation for a perceived injustice. In such a case, the attackers, having no real political aims, are little more than mass murderers. Several incidents fit this description:

- In 1986, Libya ordered an attack on a Berlin discotheque frequented by Americans to avenge the sinking of two boats by the United States. Three people were killed and more than 200 injured. Ten days later, the United States bombed Tripoli, the Libyan capital, in retaliation; at least 15 civilians died.

- In 1993, radical Muslims set off 15 bombs in Bombay that killed 250 people and injured 1,100. The bombings were meant to **retaliate** for anti-Muslim riots that left hundreds dead.

- In 1994, a Jewish physician opened fire on Muslims worshiping in a mosque in Hebron, a city in the Israeli-occupied West Bank; he killed 29 Palestinians and wounded 125. The doctor was supposedly upset by Palestinian attacks on his friends.

Before 1990, a suicide bomber was typically a young man between the ages of seventeen and twenty-two; he was uneducated, unemployed, and unmarried. In the last twenty years, however, it has become impossible to stereotype a suicide bomber. The bomber may be uneducated or a college graduate, married or single, socially isolated or well connected, and anywhere between thirteen and fifty-three years old. As of 2011, 10 to 20 percent of suicide bombers were women.

Suicide bombers are not irrational or insane. One Palestinian gave a classic defense of the tactic: "We do not have highly advanced weaponry with which to face a regular army. All we are in control of is our bodies. We do not like or want to die. But if this is what it takes to terrorize them as they brutalize us all the time, why not do it?"

Organizations usually have few problems recruiting suicide bombers. The families of those who accept the assignment receive money for their sacrifice. Radical Islamic groups also claim suicide bombers will go directly to paradise for defending the faith. The founder of Hamas compared the funeral of a suicide bomber to a wedding: "His death is

DID YOU KNOW?

Some of the worst terrorist attacks in Southeast Asia took place in hotels and nightclubs in Bali, Indonesia; many of the hundreds of people killed in 2002 and 2005 were foreign tourists.

A poster in the West Bank glorifies a Palestinian suicide bomber who killed 16 people (and himself) in 2002.

like a celebration—we offer candy, sweets, and cold drinks, because we know he'll be so high in heaven."

However, many suicide bombers are secular (the Chechens; the PKK) or belong to non-Islamic faiths (the Tamil Tigers). A young Tamil Tiger explained why he was willing to be a suicide bomber: "This is the most supreme sacrifice I can make. The only way we can get our homeland is through arms. That is the only way anybody will listen to us. Even if we die."

IS SUICIDE BOMBING EVER JUSTIFIED?

After the September 2001 attacks, the Pew Global Attitudes Survey began asking Muslims if "suicide bombing and other forms of violence against civilian targets are justified in order to defend Islam from its enemies." The numbers below represent the percentage of Muslim respondents who answered that suicide bombing is "often justified" or "sometimes justified" to defend Islam.

Muslim respondents who consider suicide bombing often or sometimes justified (%)

	2002	2005	2006	2007	2008	2009
Palestinian Territories				70		68
Nigeria	47		46	42	32	43
Lebanon	74	39		34	34	38
Indonesia	26	15	10	10	11	13
Jordan	43	57	29	23	25	12
Israel						7
Pakistan	33	25	14	9	5	5
Turkey	13	14	17	16	3	4

Source: Juliana Horowitz, "Declining Support for Bin Laden and Suicide Bombing," Pew Global Attitudes Project, September 10, 2009, http://pewresearch.org/pubs/1338/declining-muslim-support-for-bin-laden-suicide-bombing.

A female Palestinian suicide bomber with her three-year old son. She blew herself up at a checkpoint between Israel and the Gaza Strip in 2004, killing herself and four Israelis.

DID YOU KNOW?

On September 1, 2010, U.S. troops formally ended combat operations in Iraq. Less than a week before, a wave of suicide bombers killed at least 62 people and wounded hundreds in coordinated attacks on Iraqi security forces throughout the country.

WHAT DO YOU THINK?

Why do some people think that religious belief is closely related to the use of terrorist tactics? Give one piece of evidence to support this belief and one piece of evidence that contradicts it.

Why do you think some people would justify suicide bombing? Do you believe it is ever justifiable? Why or why not?

Examine the chart on page 45. What trends do you notice in the chart? Can you come up with any reasons for these trends?

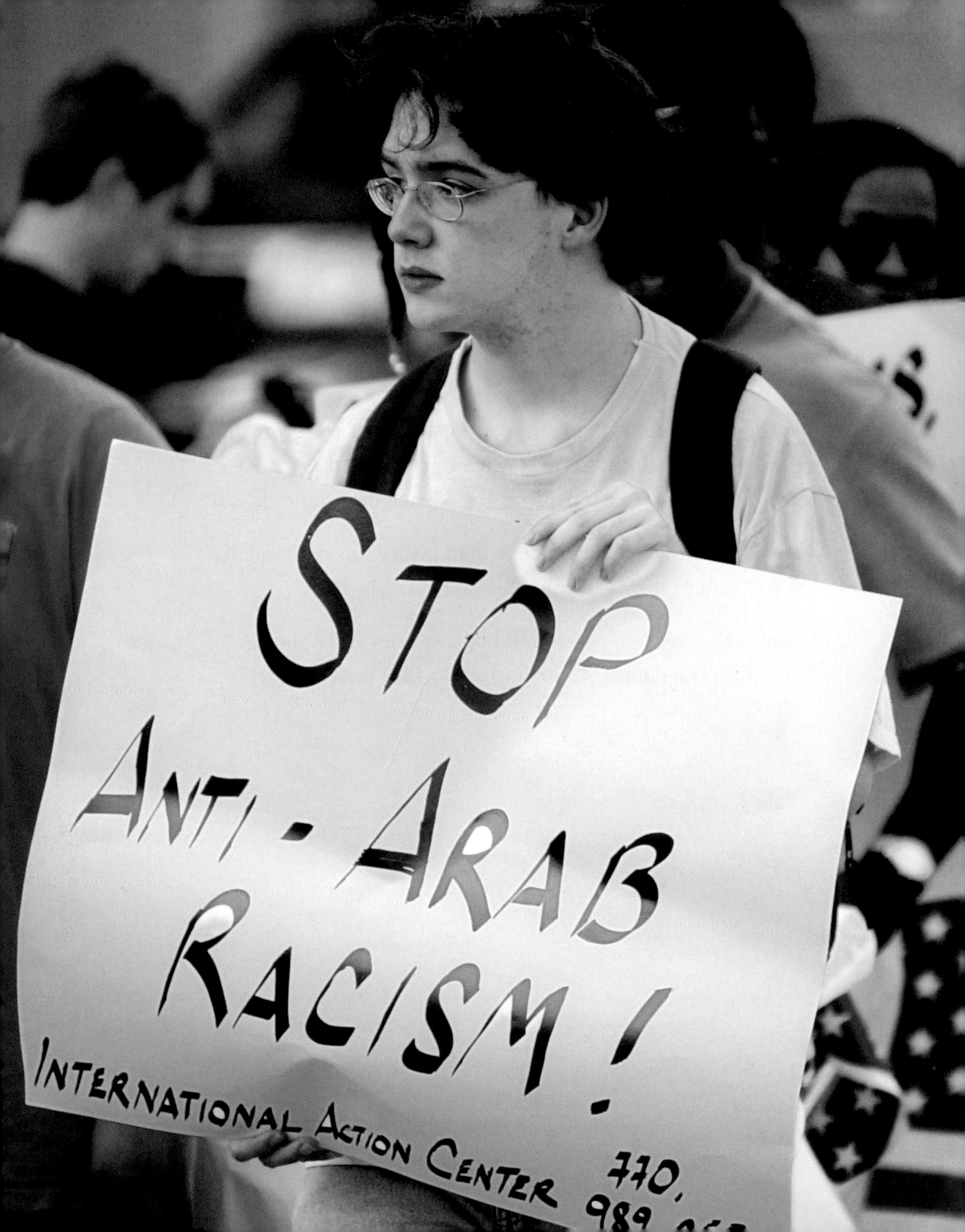
STOP
ANTI-ARAB
RACISM!
INTERNATIONAL ACTION CENTER

Chapter 4

Nations often respond to attacks by terrorists by declaring a "war on terror." Governments assert that they must defeat terrorists by using all possible means, especially military ones. They declare that emergency measures are necessary to make people safe. For example, in 2005, the Italian parliament passed an antiterrorism law allowing the police to take DNA samples from suspects without formally charging them with a crime. Sometimes these emergency measures last a long time. In Northern Ireland, the British parliament passed restrictive "emergency" laws against the IRA in 1973 that lasted more than two decades.

However, the "war" metaphor is not necessarily appropriate. Fighting terrorists is like fighting an invisible army. The concept of war is hard to apply to people who usually have no territory to defend, no capital to seize, no army to surround, and no citizens to be threatened.

Wars eventually end, but terrorism can never be eliminated. There will always be someone willing to give his or her life for a cause. Individual terrorists may be killed, but terrorism will continue. A more realistic goal would be to reduce the extent of terrorism so that it interferes as little as possible with the open ways of democracies.

The attacks against the United States in 2001 unleashed a good deal of anti-Arab prejudice. To counter that intolerance, a man holds an antiracism sign during a peace and healing rally.

The United States Responds to Terrorist Attacks

How much are people willing to sacrifice in order to feel safe? Democratic governments must try to find the difficult balance between the need of citizens to be secure and the need to protect people's civil rights. Fear and anger sometimes lead to extreme actions and the **scapegoating** of innocent people.

The U.S. Homeland Security Chief discusses the color-coded U.S. threat advisory system to deal with potential terrorist attack. The system was widely ridiculed and phased out in January 2011.

The attacks on the United States in 2001 were by far the worst terrorist attacks by a nongovernmental organization in history. The U.S. response was equally massive. President Bush promised to "root out" terrorism and "hunt down" those who were responsible. Bush said, "Every nation in every region now has a decision to make. Either you are with us, or you are with the terrorists." The Bush administration stated that the United States had the right to attack any foreign countries that represented a possible threat to the United States even if that threat was not immediate. Fighting terrorism was the American justification for invading Afghanistan in 2001 and Iraq in 2003. As of 2011, American soldiers were still fighting in Afghanistan with total casualties estimated anywhere between 100,000 and one million. (The last U.S. combat brigade withdrew from Iraq in August 2010.)

The Bush administration created the Department of Homeland Security less than a month after the attacks. The creation of this cabinet-level department was the biggest government reorganization in American history. The department's purpose is to keep the United States safe by developing a national strategy for detecting, protecting, and responding to terrorist attacks.

Also in 2001, the U.S. Congress passed the Patriot Act. This law greatly expanded the government's powers of surveillance and detention. It gave law-enforcement

DID YOU KNOW?

In 2010, the Department of Homeland Security was one of the U.S. government's largest cabinet-level departments. It had a budget of more than $40 billion, and employed about 200,000 contractors and 188,000 federal employees (not counting uniformed members of the U.S. Coast Guard).

agencies the authority to search telephone records and e-mails as well as medical, financial, and other personal records without a court order. Supporters argued that the aggressive use of informants, spying, wiretaps, searches, and interrogation were necessary to protect the country against terrorist attacks.

However, some Americans questioned the wisdom and scope of the Patriot Act. They criticized its easing of restrictions on detentions of immigrants and warrantless searches of the records of individuals, corporate entities, and public and private agencies. Modifications made to the Patriot Act during and after 2009 did not take into account these civil liberties–based objections.

Another question for the United States to resolve was the treatment of terrorism suspects. Were they entitled to prisoner of war status? In 2001, President Bush signed an executive order declaring that the suspects were "enemy combatants." In this way, the president suspended the writ of habeas corpus that guaranteed a person the right to challenge his or her imprison-

Several provisions of the 2001 Patriot Act became extremely controversial. One debate involved the government's ability to access bookstore and library records. Despite many protests, this provision was still in force as of February 2011.

ment in front of a fair authority. Instead, foreigners suspected of terrorism were to be tried in special military tribunals. There would be no jury, hearsay evidence would be permitted, and the proceedings could be held in secret. President Bush insisted that tribunals were necessary in times of war, while critics complained that Bush had seized dictatorial power and betrayed basic American values.

Other Methods to Reduce Terrorism

The most common counterterrorism strategy is to kill or capture terrorists before an attack happens. This approach has its shortcomings. If ten people are willing to take the place of every terrorist killed, attacks will not decrease no matter how many terrorists are killed. When he was Secretary of Defense, Donald Rumsfeld complained, "The United States is putting relatively little effort into a long-range plan, but we are putting a great deal of effort into trying to stop terrorists."

Acquiring information is crucial to reducing incidents of terrorism. How many people are in a terrorist group? Where do they train? What sort of weapons do they have? Do any other nations help them? Where do they get their money? Much of this intelligence gathering is done at the national level. Ideally, nations would then share their information. International cooperation makes it harder for various groups to recruit new members, obtain weapons, and raise funds from sympathizers around the world.

The most visible way to reduce terrorist attacks is to increase security around potential targets. For example, at airports people without

TORTURE AND THE U.S. WAR ON TERRORISM

In 1984, the United States helped write the Convention Against Torture (CAT). The CAT specifically states that there are "no circumstances whatsoever, whether a state of war or a threat of war . . . or any other public emergency . . . that could be invoked as a justification for torture . . . [or] other acts of cruel, inhumane or degrading treatment" in order to get prisoners to divulge information.

However, after the attacks in September 2001, the United States insisted that Al Qaeda and Taliban suspects were not entitled to the protections of the Geneva Conventions, which guarantee humane treatment of prisoners of war. For the first time in American history, government officials were allowed to physically and psychologically torment captives held by the United States. The techniques included forced nudity, painful stress positions, sleep deprivation, and waterboarding (a form of torture in which the captive is made to believe he is suffocating to death under water). In 2002, the Bush administration redefined the crime of torture to make it almost impossible to commit.

The United States also sent more than a thousand suspects and prisoners to other countries for questioning. Intelligence officials admitted they sent people to places where the security services engaged in torture.

In 2006, the U.S. Supreme Court, in *Hamdan v. Rumsfeld*, declared that even in war, the president had to follow laws and treaties, including the Geneva Conventions. Senator John McCain, the Republican candidate for president in 2008, had spent seven years in captivity in Vietnam where he had experienced torture firsthand. Regarding the scandal over American incidents of torture in 2006, McCain said,

We should not torture or treat inhumanely terrorists we have captured. The abuse of prisoners harms, not helps, our war effort. In my experience, abuse of prisoners often produces bad intelligence because under torture a person will say anything he thinks his captors want to hear—whether it is true or false—if he believes it will relieve his suffering. . . .

[Every American prisoner in Vietnam] knew and took great strength from the belief that we were different from our enemies, that we were better than them, that we, if the roles were reversed, would not disgrace ourselves by committing or approving such mistreatment of them. That faith was indispensable not only to our survival, but to our attempts to return home with honor. For without our honor, our homecoming would have had little value to us."

Waterboarding is a form of torture in which the captive is made to believe he is suffocating to death under water. In 2002, the U.S. government reversed its previous position and began using waterboarding on suspected terrorists.

Prohibited Items

You may **NOT** bring the following types of items beyond this point:

SHARP OBJECTS (such as knives or pointed scissors)

FIREARMS (such as guns or ammunition)

TOOLS (such as hammers or screwdrivers)

CLUB-LIKE ITEMS (such as billy clubs, baseball bats or golf clubs)

FLAMMABLE OR EXPLOSIVE MATERIALS (such as fireworks)

DISABLING CHEMICALS (such as mace or pepper spray)

This list is provided as a guide only and is not all-inclusive

Failure to comply may lead to criminal and/or civil prosecution

www.TSATravelTips.us
Consumer Response Center: 1-866-289-9673

Transportation Security Administration

A security sign at O'Hare Airport in Chicago. Airport searches, performed without a warrant, involve some invasion of privacy. Yet most Americans seem to accept these limits on their freedoms in the name of tighter airport security.

airline tickets can no longer go to arrival or departure gates. All passengers undergo routine luggage inspections and electronic or physical

body searches. These practices were virtually unknown in the 1970s. These searches, without a warrant, involve some invasion of privacy. Yet few citizens object to these measures.

On the other hand, critics complain about the high cost (more than $6 billion a year) and the bureaucracy (more than 45,000 airport screeners) of the airport security program. Even the best security often fails to identify contraband weapons and other dangerous items. In addition, there are an unlimited number of other potential targets for terrorists: dams, power plants, museums, schools, public transportation, restaurants, and theaters. It is impossible to protect everything against the possibility of terrorist attack. People will have to make choices.

The Dilemma of the Media

Terrorist actions are usually planned to win the attention of the news media, the public, and the government. Without media coverage, a terrorist act would be known only in the immediate area of the attack and would not reach the wider "target" audience. Some scholars have discussed terrorism as if it were a form of theater. Like an actor, a terrorist needs an audience to be successful.

Prohibited Items Intercepted at U.S. Airport Screening Checkpoints

	2003	2005	2007
Enplanements	587,535,022	660,614,523	681,492,975
TOTAL	6,114,612	15,887,596	6,516,022
Prohibited items			
Firearms	683	2,217	1,416
Knives	1,961,849	1,822,752	1,056,687
Box cutters	20,991	21,315	11,908
Other cutting instruments	2,973,413	3,276,691	101,387
Clubs	25,139	20,531	9,443
Incendiaries	494,123	398,830	89,623
Other	638,414	10,345,260	5,245,558

Source: U.S. Department of Transportation, "Prohibited Items Intercepted at Airport Screening Checkpoints," Research and Administrative Technology Association, October 2008, at http://www.bts.gov/publications/national_transportation_statistics/html/table_02_16b.html.

Modern terrorist organizations are extremely skilled at using the media, especially the Internet. One Al Qaeda leader told group members, "I say to you that we are in a battle, and that more than half of this battle is taking place in the battlefield of the media." Web content produced by many terrorist organizations is very sophisticated and professional. Al Qaeda's Internet material includes editorials, news digests, messages from Osama bin Laden, slick graphics, and even videos of the last messages of suicide bombers.

Mass media, especially television, often indirectly assist people using terrorist tactics by devoting extraordinary broadcast time and column inches to even minor violence. Through media coverage, the events of September 11, 2001, dominated every aspect of American life. In some cases, the increase in terrorism-

The Internet has become an effective way to spread radical messages. The first edition (2010) of Al Qaeda's online magazine includes articles such as "Make a Bomb in the Kitchen of your Mom."

related stories created a stronger fear and helped paralyze the nation. The stock market declined, and the flying public was so terrified that several major airlines went into **bankruptcy**. Yet it is the media's job to report the news and make a profit. The more sensational the news, the more people read or watch.

When she was prime minister of the United Kingdom, Margaret Thatcher said, regarding the IRA, that publicity is the oxygen of terrorism. She suggested the media should censor themselves and agree that, "they would not say or show anything which could assist the terrorists' morale or their cause while the hijack lasted." However, any form of **censorship** is a controversial subject in democratic societies. As of 2011, there has been no agreement as to how the media can prevent popularizing terrorist violence.

Another dilemma involves the media's role in democracies as a watchdog of the government. Studies show that a majority of the American public wants a watchdog press and at the same time expects a pro-American slant to the news. For journalists covering terrorism, this is an almost impossible balancing act. A poll in 2003 showed that seven in ten Americans thought it good coverage to have "a strong pro-American point of view." Journalists who did not deliver risked losing advertisers, audiences, and sometimes their jobs.

Faced with this dilemma, the media often become cheerleaders of the government in times of terrorist attacks. After the September 11 attacks, television news in particular emphasized the idea that being a good American meant standing united and always supporting the president. Media coverage seemed to insist that military intervention was inevitable and appropriate; very few reporters suggested that invading other countries might not succeed. However, this cheerleading did the media little good; almost half

DID YOU KNOW?

More than 200 people jumped to their deaths from the World Trade Center on September 11, 2001. The mainstream media have judged these images too disturbing to print or broadcast and refused to show them. Public opinion is mixed on this act of self-censorship. Ironically, the images and videos were easily accessed on YouTube.

of Americans polled in 2007 still faulted American press and television news for failing to stand up for the country.

WHAT DO YOU THINK?

What actions did the U.S. government take after Al Qaeda's attacks in 2001?

Louis Brandeis, a noted Supreme Court justice, said, "The greatest dangers to liberty lurk in the insidious encroachment by men of zeal, well meaning but without understanding." What do you think this statement means? Do you think it applies to the actions of the United States after 2001? Why or why not?

What dilemmas do the media face in covering terrorist attacks?

Chapter **5**

Social studies is not only concerned with things that occurred in the past. Social studies also deals with real-life problems—difficult questions without any clear solutions. No amount of memorizing facts, figures, and dates will provide the "correct" answers. Instead, people who use **critical thinking** carefully analyze situations and suspend judgment until all available data has been gathered and considered.

Below are three modern-day situations involving terrorism. Two remained unresolved at the time of the printing of this book. What would you do if the decision were up to you—you decide!

Should Governments Negotiate with Groups Accused of Terrorism?

Governments usually resist talking to groups accused of terrorism. They fear negotiating as equals will reward violence and spread the message that the path to political recognition is through the murder of civilians. People who oppose negotiations claim the willingness of democracies to make concessions has inspired terrorist tactics. They believe that compromise is impossible because terrorists see the world in black and

There will probably always be someone willing to give his or her life for a cause. However, perhaps it is possible to reduce the extent of terrorism so it interferes as little as possible with the open ways of democracies.

CASE STUDY #1

The Islamic resistance organization known as Hamas demands the "liberation" of Palestine from the Mediterranean Sea to the Jordan River. Many members of Hamas deny Israel's right to exist as a nation. Between 1993 and 2005, Hamas organized several large suicide bombings against Israeli civilian targets and attacked Israeli cities using mortars and short-range rockets.

In January 2006, Hamas won a large majority in an election to the Palestinian parliament and has governed the Gaza part of the Palestinian territories (through 2011). Hamas's continued refusal to recognize the state of Israel has led to crippling economic sanctions against Palestine by Israel and the United States. Hamas is still described as a terrorist organization by the governments of the United States, the European Union, Israel, Japan, and Canada.

The United States and Israel refuse to negotiate with Hamas. Yet many difficult Middle Eastern issues remain unresolved, including the right of Palestinians to their own nation, the right of Israel to build settlements on land claimed by Palestinians, and the status of Jerusalem.

YOU DECIDE

- Should the Israeli or United States government negotiate with Hamas?

- Refuse to negotiate at any time with Hamas because it is a terrorist group.

- Negotiate with Hamas if it accepts certain preconditions, such as the right of Israel to exist.

- Hold secret negotiations with Hamas while maintaining an official policy of refusing to talk to the group.

- Open low-level contacts with Hamas but refuse to negotiate formally until preconditions are met.

- Open formal negotiations with Hamas.

- Would it affect your decision if Hamas had not won the popular election in Gaza in 2006?

Hamas supporters, carrying fake rockets and wearing replica bombs wrapped around their waists (simulating a suicide bomber), parade down a street in Gaza in 2001.

- Would it affect your decision if popular opinion in Israel favored or opposed negotiating with Hamas?

ACTUAL OUTCOME

As of October 1, 2010, the United States and Israel had refused to negotiate with Hamas; there were subsequent signs this refusal was being reconsidered.

white. According to this philosophy, overwhelming force is the only way to deal with organizations that use terrorist tactics.

However, some people support negotiating with terrorist groups. They believe the refusal to **negotiate** sounds like an extremely moral position but ignores practical realities. The refusal to negotiate wastes opportunities to create real change. Sometimes the refusal to negotiate can isolate an organization and allow the conflict to last even longer. Negotiation supporters insist there is never any harm in talking.

Tony Blair, the UK's prime minister (1997–2007), distinguished between when and when not to negotiate. Blair said the demands of the Irish Republican Army for Northern Ireland, thought by many to be a terrorist group, "are demands that would be shared by many perfectly law-abiding people. . . ." On the other hand, the demands of Al Qaeda were "none that any serious person could ever negotiate on." Negotiations between the British government and the IRA did help lead to at least temporary peace in Northern Ireland.

Are Strike Forces the Best Way to Deal with Hostage Situations?

One antiterrorism tactic is the development of strike forces—military or police units specially trained and equipped to combat terrorism and to rescue hostages. There are many conflicting views on whether these are useful tools in fighting terrorist actions. The possibility of success has to be measured against the cost of failure.

Strike forces and rescue teams have had mixed results. In 1976, an

CASE STUDY #2

September 1, 2004, was a traditional holiday in Russia celebrating the start of the school year. On that day, about 30 heavily armed masked men entered a middle school and took more than 1,100 hostages in Beslan, in the area of North Ossetia. More than 700 of the hostages were children from six to sixteen years of age. The hostage takers demanded formal independence for Chechnya and the withdrawal of Russian troops from the area.

Hostage taking allows groups to maximize the publicity surrounding an event. Hostage takers can often control the length of the event and the media coverage. This is appealing to people looking for wider publicity for their action. At Beslan, the taking of the hostages led to a tense two-day standoff. The hostage takers killed several people and threatened to shoot many more if a rescue was attempted.

YOU DECIDE

- How should the Russian government respond to the situation in Beslan?

- Give the hostage takers everything they want; the lives of 1,100 hostages are more important than holding on to Chechnya.

- Pretend to negotiate while planning an attack on the school that will not lead to too many deaths.

- Negotiate in good faith and try to find a common ground that will spare all lives.

- Treat the hostages as if they were already dead and attack the school in order to set the precedent that there will be no negotiations with terrorists.

- Would it affect your decision if you knew that two years earlier, Chechen fighters had seized a theater in Moscow and taken 700 hostages? A rescue attempt was not well organized or executed, and more than 120 people died.

- Would it affect your decision if the hostages were adults rather than schoolchildren?

- Would it affect your decision if the hostage takers demanded the release of 200 Chechens held in Russian jails instead of independence for Chechnya?

ACTUAL OUTCOME

On the third day of the standoff, Russian forces stormed the school using tanks, rockets, flamethrowers, and other heavy weapons. There is still dispute whether the Russian security forces began the attack themselves or felt compelled to enter the school to save the hostages. By the time the fighting ended two hours later, about 330 hostages had been killed, including 186 children.

The 2004 attack is still controversial. Critics say that the storming of the school was unnecessary and led to the death of the hostages. They insist that more could have been done to negotiate the release of

In 2004, Chechen separatists took more than 1,000 hostages at a school in Beslan, Russia. An estimated 330 people were killed, including 186 children, in a controversial rescue attempt. Here, a woman stands next to a wall with portraits of people killed in the incident.

the hostages. They complain that the Russian government has covered up the causes of the tragedy to protect senior members of the security services. Defenders of the action insist that no other solution was possible to deal with ruthless and stubborn terrorists. They insist the Russians security forces were heroes who saved the lives of hundreds of hostages.

Israeli commando team freed 256 hostages (4 were killed) and killed the Palestinian hijackers of an Air France jet in Entebbe, Uganda. In 1996, the Peruvian government cleverly used underground tunnels built by professional miners to rescue all but 1 of 72 hostages held by the Túpac Amaru group for four months at the Japanese ambassador's residence in Lima.

However, sometimes these rescue attempts turn into disasters, as the German response to the hostage taking at the Munich Olympics in 1972 did. Another failed attempt occurred in 1980, when the United States attempted to send a strike team into Iran to free hostages held by the Iranian government. The mission failed when two helicopters collided and nine people died.

How Should the United States Respond to State Terrorism?

State terrorism has killed many more people than nongovernmental terrorist groups. State terrorism occurs when a government uses the police, judges, and military against its own people to prevent any opposition. However, state terrorism is extremely difficult to deal with because nations are independent units, and intervention will often lead to war.

CASE STUDY #3

In December 2008, Captain Mousse Dadis Camara took power in a military coup in Guinea, a mineral-rich country in western Africa. Camara promised he would not run for reelection but then changed his mind. Many people from Guinea were outraged and held a rally in September 2009 to protest Camara's decision to run again. Almost 50,000 protesters met in a stadium in Conakry, the nation's capital. The government's troops invaded the rally and went on a brutal rampage. They shot, stabbed, raped, and assaulted dozens of unarmed men and women in the packed stadium in broad daylight. Human rights groups in Guinea reported that at least 150 people were killed and about 1,000 injured in the attacks. Camara barely apologized for the deaths and tried to shift the blame to the protesters.

The United Nations, European Union, and African Union condemned the massacre in the Conakry stadium. France, the former colonial master of Guinea, announced that it was suspending military aid. The African Union and the European Union imposed a travel ban and froze any bank accounts owned by high-ranking members of the government.

YOU DECIDE

- How should the United States respond to the situation in Guinea?
- Ignore the situation completely. The violence is not a threat to the United States. What happens in someone else's country is that country's business.

- Make a statement in the United Nations condemning the violence and then ignore it.

- Use diplomacy to encourage the Economic Community of West African States (ECOWAS) to intervene economically in Guinea.

- Use diplomacy to encourage the ECOWAS to intervene militarily in Guinea.

- Cut off all American imports and exports to Guinea until the government resigns.

More than 150 people were killed and 1,000 injured in brutal attacks by the Guinean government on unarmed protesters in a stadium in Conakry, Guinea, in 2009. Here, a Guinean police officer arrests a protester in front of the stadium.

- Invade Guinea, depose Camara, and put the opposition in power.

- What other information would you like to have?

- Would it affect your decision if Guinea were a major trading partner of the United States?

- Would it affect your decision if Guinea had vast oil reserves?

- Would it affect your decision if Guinea were a longtime ally of the United States?

- Would it affect your decision if 10,000 people had been killed in the stadium?

ACTUAL OUTCOME

The United States imposed targeted travel restrictions and expressed support for a new democratic government. The U.S. Congress officially condemned Camara's actions. In December 2009, Camara was wounded in an assassination attempt and left the country. Months of tension and unrest followed. It was agreed that elections would be held and the military would not contest them. These would be the first democratic elections in Guinea since 1958, but as of early 2011, they had been postponed several times and the situation had not been resolved.

Timeline

Discussed in this book since the 1972 Munich Olympics

1972 — Twelve people are killed by Palestinian terrorists at the Summer Olympics in Munich, Germany.

1976 — Israel dispatches a commando team that frees 256 hostages (4 killed) and kills Palestinian hijackers of an Air France jet in Entebbe, Uganda.

1979 — In an armed attack by Muslim extremists on the Grand Mosque in Mecca, Saudi Arabia, more than 200 are killed and 600 wounded.

1983 — Using trucks, suicide bombers blow up buildings housing French and U.S. military forces in Lebanon; 250 soldiers are killed.

1985 — Tamil Tigers kill 146 Sinhalese people with automatic weapons in Anuradhapura, Sri Lanka.

1985 — Sikh separatists bomb an Air India flight off Ireland; 329 people are killed.

1986 — Libyan agents bomb a discotheque in Berlin; 3 people are killed and more than 200 are wounded.

1987 — North Korean agents explode a bomb on Korean Air Flight 858; all 115 on board are killed.

1988 — Libyan agents bomb Pan Am Flight 103 over Lockerbie, Scotland; 270 are killed.

1993 — Fundamentalist Muslims explode a truck bomb in the basement of the World Trade Center in New York City; 6 people are killed and 1,000 are wounded.

1995 — American terrorist kills 168 people in a truck bombing of the Alfred P. Murrah Federal Building in Oklahoma City.

1995 — The Japanese cult Aum Shinrikyo kills 12 and injures 5,500 in a nerve gas attack in the Tokyo subway system.

1996 — Tamil Tigers ram a truck loaded with explosives into the Central Bank in Colombo, Sri Lanka; 91 people are killed and 1,400 are wounded.

1996 — The Peruvian government uses underground tunnels to rescue all but 1 of 72 hostages held by the Túpac Amaru group for four months at the Japanese ambassador's residence in Lima.

1998 — Two U.S. embassies, in Nairobi, Kenya, and Dar es Salaam, Tanzania, are attacked by Al Qaeda suicide bombers; 303 are killed and 4,000 are wounded.

1998 – A splinter group of the IRA opposed to the Belfast Agreement organizes a car bomb attack in Omagh, Northern Ireland; 29 are killed and 220 are injured.

1999 – The bombing of an apartment building in Moscow, Russia, by Chechen separatists kills 130 and wounds 150.

2001 – Members of Al Qaeda crash hijacked planes into the World Trade Center, in New York City; the Pentagon, in Virginia; and a site in Pennsylvania; 2,993 are killed and almost 9,000 are wounded.

2002 – Chechen separatists attack a theater in Moscow; a failed rescue attempt results in 170 deaths.

2002 – Jemaah Islamiyah, a Southeast Asian Islamic organization with links to Al Qaeda, kills 200 and wounds 350 by exploding three bombs outside a nightclub in Kuta, on the island of Bali, in Indonesia.

2004 – Al Qaeda supporters bomb the Atocha train station in Madrid; 191 are killed and more than 600 are injured.

2004 – Chechen separatists take hostages at a school in Beslan, Russia; 330 are killed and more than 700 are injured.

2004 – Muslim groups allied with Al Qaeda set off a bomb on a Philippine ferry near Manila; 116 people are killed.

2005 – Four Al Qaeda suicide bombers target the public transportation system in London; 56 are killed and more than 700 are injured.

2005 – Suicide bombers associated with Iraq targeted Western hotels in Amman, Jordan; 60 are killed and 110 are injured.

2006 – Lashkar-e-Taiba, a South Asian Muslim organization, organizes multiple bombings on commuter trains in Mumbai, India; 209 are killed and more than 700 are wounded.

2008 – Lashkar-e-Taiba organizes multiple shootings, grenade attacks, and hostage takings in Mumbai, India; 160 are killed and 370 are wounded.

2009 – More than 150 people are killed and more than 1,000 are injured in an attack by the Guinean government on unarmed protesters in a stadium in Conakry, Guinea.

2010 – Suicide bombers kill more than 70 people and wound about 400 in attacks on Shiite pilgrims converging on a shrine in northern Baghdad.

2011 – On May 1, Osama bin Laden was killed in a raid carried out by U.S. Navy SEALs in Abbottabad, Pakistan.

Glossary

aggressor—A person or country that attacks another person or country, sometimes without cause.

ambush—A surprise attack made from a hidden position.

anarchist—A person who supports anarchism, the belief that almost all forms of government reduce individual freedom and should be abolished.

assassin—A murderer who, for political reasons, uses a surprise attack to kill an important or famous person.

bankruptcy—A legally declared condition when a person or organization cannot pay its debts.

censorship—Restrictions placed on books, movies, or other media that involve the removal of material considered improper or harmful.

civilian—Any member of a society who is not serving in the armed forces.

conventional war—A war in which only conventional (that is, nonnuclear) weapons are used.

counterterrorism—Strategies used by governmental or private organizations to prevent or counteract terrorism.

critical thinking—The process of closely evaluating information to discover underlying issues and other matters that are not readily apparent.

hijack—To seize control of a vehicle or airplane in transit.

hostage—A person who is held captive, generally to serve as security that a specific demand will be met.

jihad—Usually, a war against nonbelievers waged by Muslims.

martyr—A person who chooses to die rather than betray a belief, cause, or principle.

Marxist—A person who believes in the theories of Karl Marx—that fighting between economic classes will eventually change capitalism to communism.

minority—A group within a country or area that differs in race, religion, or national origin from the larger group of which it is a part.

nationalist—One who advocates a strong national government or national independence.

negotiate—To talk about something in the hope of resolving a dispute.

nerve gas—A toxic gas, inhaled or absorbed through the skin, that paralyzes the central nervous system. It usually causes death by asphyxiation.

noncombatant—In wartime, a civilian or a nonfighting member of the armed forces.

oppression—A condition in which authority is exercised in a harsh or unjust manner.

retaliate—To fight back or respond to an injury or insult.

scapegoat—A person, group, or thing that is assigned the blame for things done by others.

tactic—A plan or maneuver for achieving a goal.

Find Out More

Books

Combs, Cindy. *Terrorism in the Twenty-First Century*, 5th ed. Upper Saddle River, NJ: Prentice Hall, 2008.

Freedman, Jeri. *America Debates Civil Liberties and Terrorism*. New York: Rosen Central, 2008.

Hiber, Amanda. *Should Governments Negotiate with Terrorists?* Detroit: Greenhaven Press, 2008.

Stefoff, Rebecca. *Security vs. Privacy* (Open for Debate). New York: Marshall Cavendish Benchmark, 2008.

Weinberg, Leonard. *What Is Terrorism?* New York: Chelsea House, 2006.

Websites

United Nations Office on Drugs and Crime. "UNODC and Terrorism Prevention," 2009

www.unodc.org/unodc/en/terrorism/index.html

U.S. Department of Homeland Security

www.dhs.gov/index.shtm

Council of Foreign Relations

www.cfr.org

Index
Page numbers in boldface are illustrations.

About the Author

Jon Sterngass is the author of *First Resorts: Pursuing Pleasure at Saratoga Springs, Newport, and Coney Island* (2001). He currently is a freelance writer specializing in children's nonfiction books. He has written more than forty books; among his recent works are biographies of Frederick Douglass and Geronimo and a history of Filipino Americans. Born and raised in Brooklyn, Jon Sterngass has a BA from Franklin and Marshall College, an MA in medieval history from the University of Wisconsin–Milwaukee, and a PhD in nineteenth-century American history from the City University of New York. He has lived in Saratoga Springs, New York, for sixteen years with his wife, Karen Weltman, and their sons, Eli and Aaron.